Fantasy & Legend
Scroll Saw Puzzles

by Judy and Dave Peterson

Fox Chapel
PUBLISHING

Dedication

This book is dedicated to all of the customers whose suggestions I've adopted.

Fantasy & Legend Scroll Saw Puzzles is an original work, first published in 2005 by Fox Chapel Publishing Company, Inc. The patterns contained herein are copyrighted by the author. Readers may make three copies of these patterns for personal use. The patterns themselves, however, are not to be duplicated for resale or distribution under any circumstances. Any such copying is a violation of copyright law.

ISBN: 978–1–56523–256–3

Publisher's Cataloging-in-Publication Data

Peterson, Judy.
     Fantasy & legend scroll saw puzzles / by Judy and Dave Peterson. --
     East Petersburg, PA : Fox Chapel Publishing, c2005.

          p. ; cm.

          Includes index.
          ISBN-13: 978–1–56523–256–3
          ISBN-10: 1–56523–256–9

          1. Jigsaw puzzles. 2. Wooden novelties. 3. Woodwork--Patterns.
I. Peterson, Dave. II. Title. III. Fantasy and legend scroll saw puzzles.

TT174.5.W6 P48 2005
745.592--dc22   0501

To learn more about the other great books from Fox Chapel Publishing, or to find a retailer near you, call toll-free 800-457-9112 or visit us at *www.FoxChapelPublishing.com*.

Note to Authors: We are always looking for talented authors to write new books. Please send a brief letter describing your idea to Acquisition Editor, 1970 Broad Street, East Petersburg, PA 17520.

Printed in China
Fourth printing

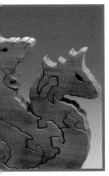

Table of Contents

About the Authors

A former schoolteacher and librarian, Judy found her niche in life as a woodworker. She bought her first saw in 1990 and, within the first six months, was cutting and creating her own designs. A winner of many design awards, Judy now sells her puzzles at art and craft shows around the country. She has also written several articles featuring her puzzles for Scroll Saw Workshop magazine, and she teaches scroll sawing at the Woodcraft store in her hometown of Madison, Wisconsin. In her spare time, Judy reads, keeps track of politics on TV, gardens, cooks, turns bowls on her lathe, and puts together other people's flat puzzles.

Dave is a senior systems analyst for a small mail order company. His interest in, and experience with, computers, databases, and spreadsheets makes him suited to run the record-keeping side of Judy's small business. In his spare time, Dave reads, is active in the local Macintosh Users' Group, writes occasional articles for the Wisconsin Alliance of Artists and Craftspeople (WAAC) newsletter, and tries to keep up with his wife.

When working on books and magazine articles, Judy does all the designing, scrollwork, sanding, and finishing. She also writes all the technical portions. Dave organizes the material, scans the patterns and takes photos.

This book is the result of their second collaboration. Fox Chapel Publishing published their first book, *Dinosaur Puzzles for the Scroll Saw*, in August 2002.

Introduction

Why interlocking and freestanding puzzles?

I like puzzles. These days, when I'm not making my own puzzles, I'm likely to be assembling someone else's. I didn't, however, plan to go into business designing and making jigsaw puzzles. I bought a scroll saw because I have always liked wood and because I was fascinated by the scroll saw work I saw at an art show. In 1989, when my family and I made our annual trek to a nearby Renaissance Fair, I bought a five-piece puzzle as a souvenir. While it was attractive, it was not interlocking, so you really couldn't pick it up.

When I began designing my own puzzles, I decided all of them would be interlocking, so that they could be handled. The puzzles in this book reflect that decision I made in 1990—all of them are interlocking. This means that, once you have the puzzles in a standing position, you can pick them up by any piece and turn them completely around without having them fall apart. But, you have to make sure you keep them vertical and don't tip them!

The first thing I cut out when I brought home that wonderful new toy, my first scroll saw, was a three-piece rabbit. As a woodworker of long standing, I used lumber I had in my workshop. It was an old piece of 1" x 4" pine. One of the things I liked about the puzzle was that it was thick enough to stand. The concept of a "freestanding" puzzle stayed with me as I moved on to using hardwoods.

Why fantasy creatures?

I bought my first copy of Edith Hamilton's *Mythology* when I was about ten. I've been reading it ever since and have branched off into science fiction and fantasy. Most of the creatures in this book are from Greek mythology with a few additions from European folklore, as well as some Chinese dragons.

The Welsh Dragon (featured on the cover and in the step-by-step section on page 6) was one of the first fantasy creatures I designed.

Like many of my subsequent designs, it resulted from a would-be customer request. A woman approached my table at one of the first shows I did, looked things over, and asked, "Do you have a Welsh dragon?" "I don't know," I replied, "what's a Welsh dragon look like?" "I don't know either," she said, "but my husband is Welsh and, if you had one, I'd buy it."

That incident sent me to the library, where I quickly found a picture of the Welsh flag, complete with dragon. I designed this pattern from the flag and liked it so well that I use it as the logo for my business.

Deciding what to design next got easier once I started selling my puzzles because people told me what their interests were. (If you're going to design a new puzzle, you might as well design one that people are likely to buy.) Customers continued to ask for fantasy puzzles, which reinforced my own interest in them. Their requests, combined with my own interests, gave me a powerful reason for designing new fantasy puzzles.

Why hardwoods?

1. They're naturally beautiful. As a lover of hardwoods, I have a natural aversion to painting them because they're beautiful in their own right. Besides that, hardwoods occur naturally in a wide variety of colors. Why cut a Welsh dragon out of a piece of pine and then paint it, when you can cut it from a red-colored wood?

2. The harder the wood, the less chip-out you get. The structure of hardwoods appears to be more uniform. Uniform density makes your cutting more consistent. You'll spend less time overall and end up with a more pleasing result.

3. The increased density also results in a surface that can be more easily sanded to a silky, smooth finish. To paraphrase something we said in our first book, *Dinosaur Puzzles for the Scroll Saw*: silky translates into sales at an art show.

Where can you buy hardwoods?

Look in the yellow pages of your phone book under "Hardwood Lumber Dealers." Ask your woodworking friends. Check out the ads in your favorite scroll sawing or woodworking magazine; some of these magazines may be available at your local library, specialty wood-working retailers, or bookstore. Keep your eyes open as you drive through unfamiliar areas. We're on the road a lot, driving to and from shows, and we found one of our best and most reliable suppliers in Ohio that way. If you have access to the Internet, use a search engine to find "Hardwood Lumber Dealers."

For more information about wood, your local public library is the source that's available to everyone. If you have a home computer, the door to almost unlimited information is open to you. This is especially true if you also have access to the Internet. Here are a few of the resources available to those with access to computers and the Internet:

www.windsorplywood.com – An amazing site, giving information on the wood from hundreds of different trees.

www.woodworkerssource.net – Another great site with information on fewer trees; however, each entry includes a colored picture of the cut lumber.

How do I choose wood for color and cutting characteristics?

I try to choose woods that are suitable for the item being cut. For instance, the Pegasus is traditionally white. Consequently, I cut most of my Pegasus puzzles from aspen or maple. I also pay attention to my customers. I sell more dragons in red woods than I do in any other color, so I often use red woods for dragons.

Almost every puzzle has a wood in which it sells best. I know that I might not have found the perfect wood for a particular pattern yet, and that knowledge keeps me searching for new and wonderful woods.

I cut most of my puzzles from cherry, maple, and walnut. Cherry appears to be the wood of choice, at the moment, but walnut is gaining popularity. I also use a smaller amount of aspen, which is usually available locally. From time to time, I find sweet gum, mesquite, sassafras, and other regionally grown woods to use for my puzzles. For the fantasy creatures, I also use chakte kok, lacewood, bocote, maca-caubo, peroba rosa, padauk, as well as many others in lesser quantities.

Many truly beautiful woods are too hard, or almost too hard, to cut with a scroll saw. Most of the woods that are "too hard" are exotics. When I run across a new species, I pick up a board. If it's heavier than a similar-sized board of hard maple, I put it back.

I always look for color and figure in every board I buy. I want the richest color for that species, and I want any figure I can find— wavy, quilted, fiddleback, etc. It's helpful to learn "Lumberspeak." (See the "Puzzling it out" tip box, page 18.) I also like to look for boards that show the contrast between heartwood and sapwood. (See page 56 in the Gallery section.) On the Hippogriff, the light-colored wood is the sapwood, and the dark-colored wood is the heartwood.

What are some of the advantages and disadvantages of various hardwoods?

The biggest disadvantage of hardwoods is price. Most hardwoods are more expensive than most softwoods. However, you don't have to buy 87 kinds of paint and spend the time painting your projects or learning to paint if you're using hardwoods.

The biggest advantage of hardwoods is beauty. With careful selection, you can produce a really good-looking puzzle.

There is one characteristic of hardwoods that's both an advantage and a disadvantage: the hardness. It takes longer to cut a puzzle in hardwood, but the finished piece is stronger. This is a great selling point for children's toys (and for puzzles for clumsy adults).

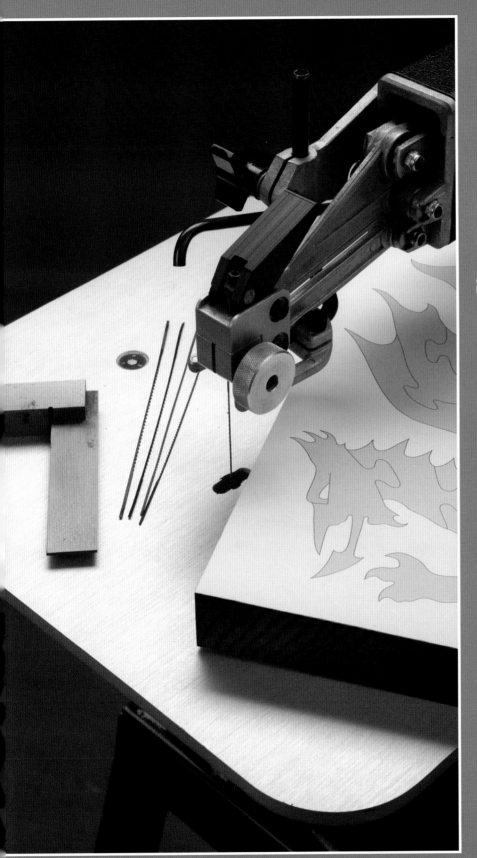

1

Getting Started

Safety

It should come as no surprise that cutting thick wood generates a lot of sawdust. Nor should it come as a surprise that breathing sawdust is not good for you. In my workshop, I have a dust collector and an air cleaner. The dust collector picks up the large particles and many of the small ones. Even if you have a dust collector, however, the air in your workshop will still have lots of tiny particles floating around. My air cleaner is mounted on the ceiling and removes a high percentage of the particles that the dust collector misses. Beyond using those two machines, I wear a dust mask that uses replaceable filters.

Eye protection is a must! I was in fifth grade when I got my first pair of glasses. Because I can't find a company that makes the kind of safety glasses I want and because I can't see well enough to work without my regular glasses, I use my regular glasses for much of my woodworking. However, my regular glasses have titanium frames and hardened lenses. When I'm sanding, I wear side shields. These translucent plastic devices slide onto your frames and keep flying particles from hitting your eyes from the side. They are available at most vision centers. Whatever type of eye protection you use in your workshop should include side shielding. If you don't need prescription lenses, use safety goggles.

You'll also do a better job of cutting and be safer if your saw has a good, well-running dust blower. This device, of course, blows the dust away from your cut line. I call this a safety issue because, before I had a blower, I reached up without thinking, to wipe the dust away from the cut line, and cut myself! Don't let it happen to you.

Also make sure that you have enough light in your workshop so that you can see what you're doing. I have two swing-arm lamps (widely available anywhere lamps are sold) mounted on my saw. These lamps come with clamps, and you can usually find somewhere to attach them if you don't have a mount for them on your saw. I find that I can cut longer with light coming from both sides. This setup also eliminates shadows and a good amount of eyestrain. You need adequate light for every-thing else you do in the workshop, too.

I also wear a hearing protector. If you're into serious woodworking, you would be well advised to at least invest in a mask, eye protection, some type of hearing protection, and possibly a dust collector.

Figure 1.
Squaring the Blade.

A word about saws

I have owned four different brands of saws and have used several others. Although it's easier to cut anything with a great, big, expensive, production-quality saw, all of these patterns have been cut with a cheap, rickety, difficult machine. Just keep practicing.

I have never seen a saw with a truly accurate degree gauge. To be sure your table is square to the blade, get a square and use it to level the table. Check your squareness if you have trouble cutting a true vertical.

To check that the blade is square to the table, lift the saw arm up as far as it will go and place the square next to it. Place a white piece of paper behind it to allow yourself to see the blade and the edge of the square as clearly as possible. (See **Figure 1.**) If the edge of the square is not perfectly parallel to the blade, your table is not level. Adjust the table accordingly.

PARTS OF THE KEY

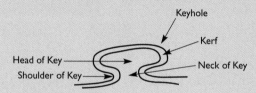

Figure 2. Parts of a Key.

Cutting on the line

Cutting on the line is fairly important on the outer edges of the puzzle. It's very important for facial features and is sometimes important on the inner cuts.

If you wobble on the outside edge of a puzzle, you can either re-cut it or ignore it. If you get off the line on the feature cuts, *stop*. Look at where you are and see if the cut can be saved. If it can, try to do so. If it can't, throw the puzzle out and try again.

On the interior (or interlocking) cuts, accuracy is not terribly important. What is important is the shape of the key. In order for the key not to pull out of the keyhole, the head of the key must be larger than the neck of the key. It also must be balanced so that there is material on both sides of the neck.

On puzzles with large pieces, there is a lot of room for error. The smaller and more complex the pieces, the more important accuracy is. See **Figure 2**, which shows how to cut the key, as well as how it is designed.

Pattern classifications

Three-dimensional puzzles are much more difficult for young children than flat puzzles with the same number of pieces. With three-dimensional puzzles, there are small muscle control issues involved. That's why I advise people not to give a more complicated puzzle to a young child. **Also note that some of the puzzles in this book contain swallowable pieces! It is critical that none of those puzzles are within the reach of children under the age of three.** Here's the easy way to tell: if a piece will pass through the hole in a roll of bathroom tissue, the piece is swallowable.

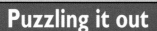

Puzzling it out

Preventing burn marks

Burn marks are a frequent problem when cutting light-colored hardwoods. After gluing the pattern in place, cover the pattern with a clear plastic sealing tape. The heat generated by the friction of the saw blade causes the plastic tape to melt. This lubricates the cut and almost eliminates burn marks.

Clear plastic sealing tape is available at department stores, office supply stores, grocery stores, and lumberyards, just to name a few. You want 2" clear plastic tape without the Mylar strands. By following this tip, I can even cut purpleheart without leaving (many) burn marks.

I cut this cherry puzzle without covering the pattern with 2" plastic tape. This piece is external, so I had quite a bit of sanding to do to get rid of the burn mark.

Easy – The puzzles categorized as "Easy" are simple in comparison to the others in this book. I consider the Welsh Dragon easy to cut, but it has breakable pieces. I would avoid giving it to any child who is rough with his/her toys.

Intermediate – These are a little more challenging to cut.

Advanced – These are even more challenging to cut. I consider the Green Man puzzle to be the most difficult one in this book.

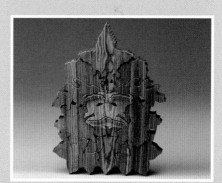

Landscape Puzzles – These differ from the other puzzles in that they represent scenes with landscape elements. They are more difficult to put together (as well as to cut) than most of the others.

Welsh Dragon.
Peroba rosa, approximately 6" tall.
This is the traditional red dragon of Wales.

Cutting a Welsh Dragon
Step-by-Step

I teach scroll sawing at my local Woodcraft store. Many of my students are just getting started, so I developed a practice pattern for them. (See page 19.). Maybe you'll want practice before you tackle some of the patterns in this book. If so, copy the pattern, glue it to a piece of scrap lumber, and practice away!

Before you can cut a puzzle out, of course, you must select the board you want to use. Examine the board carefully, looking for bad spots, including checks, knotholes, and obvious internal cracks. Mark these flaws on the top of your board. I use a wide, black permanent marker for this task.

Make a copy of the pattern you've chosen and decide where to position it on the board. Avoid the bad spots when positioning your pattern. Spray the pattern with repositionable spray adhesive and apply the pattern to the board. (See the "Puzzling it out" tip box on page 12 for information on building a glue box.)

Be sure that the adhesive you choose is "repositionable." If the label on a product doesn't include that word, you don't want to use that product for this purpose. The bond from a non-repositionable adhesive will be so secure that you'll have to spend time sanding the pattern off the pieces. However, patterns glued with repositionable spray adhesive peel off leaving no residue. (Hint: The longer you wait to peel the pattern off, the harder it will be to do so.) I've had good luck with Duro All-Purpose Spray Adhesive, available at Kmart and Wal-Mart stores, as well as many lumberyards.

My dragon heads are complicated and subject to breaking while cutting. It's my practice to start cutting at the head of a dragon. Then, if I blow it, I can peel the remainder of the puzzle off and use the board for something else.

For best results, don't use a board less than ⅞" thick or more than 1" thick for this puzzle. I used a board of peroba rosa.

Tools and Supplies

Scroll saw with dust blower	Flat trays
Skip tooth or reverse tooth blades (#5, #7, #9)	Glue box
Spray adhesive	Metal tray
2" Square	Paper towels
Clear 2" packing tape	Plastic bags, gallon resealable
Disk pad	Rubber gloves
Drill with variable speed lock	Rubber finger pads
Drill stand	Board of appropriate dimensions and ⅞" to 1" thick
Sanding disks	Dremel or other rotary power tool
Flap sander	Split mandrel for grasping sandpaper
220-grit sandpaper	Danish oil
	Various stains, if desired

Puzzling it out

Backing out
Most of the cut line detail I use involves cutting in and backing out of that cut. It takes some practice, but the trick is to relax. Pull gently back along your cut line and don't try to overcontrol the direction. Practice on a curved cut (or several).

Cutting sharp points
There are two ways to cut a sharp point. If you have the skill to do so, you can simply make the sharp turn. The other possibility is to make a turn in the waste (assuming there is waste beyond the point you're cutting).

Cutting eyes
I've devised a variety of shapes for eyes. All of them have an access cut. From there you follow the line. If the eye is a simple hole—round, square, diamond, or half circle—just cut it. Some of my puzzles have eyebrow cuts. I usually cut the eye hole first, then back out (or turn around) and cut the eyebrow.

1 Start cutting the underside of the nose of the dragon.

2 Continue around the tongue (the arrow-shaped bit)…

3 …and to the bottom of the chin.

4 Notice how my hands change position with every change in cutting angle.

5 Cut the key at the base of the head. Then, go around and up the back of the head.

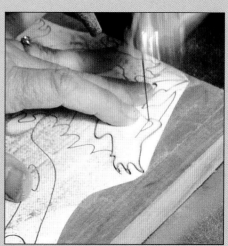

6 Cut the points and proceed to the eye. Cut down the eye line and along the base of the eye. Back out (See the "Puzzling it out" tip box, above.) to the point shown above. Turn and cut up, over, and down to the base line.

7 Remove the scrap. Then, start the saw again, back out to the top of the eye cut, and cut down to the starting point at the tip of the nose. Be sure to remove all of the scrap and finished pieces as you cut them free. If you don't, small bits will hang up in the blade slot of your table when you least expect it and when it's hardest to get them out. Always turn the saw off when removing pieces!

8 Remove the head. Note that the photo shows more than just the head removed. Before taking this photo, I had cut down the chest line and around to the claws of the first leg. Once you have removed the head, peel the pattern off, and set the piece aside. After the head, I normally cut out the feet and then the long body part.

9 Follow the chest line and continue around the first leg.

10 Notice how I'm turning in the waste to create a sharp point. Cut out both legs and remove them.

11 Here, I have cut out and removed the second leg and am starting on the third. Remove each piece as you free it, and peel off the pattern. The blower is working on my saw, but it doesn't clear enough dust away to give me good visibility. Therefore, I brush the dust off after removing each piece and in between as necessary. I recommend you do likewise. Turn the saw off first!

12 I like to assemble the puzzle as I cut out each piece. This gives me a chance to verify that the cuts were vertical. If there's a problem, the sooner you identify it, the sooner you can correct it. After you have cut around the outside of the third foot, you'll need to turn around in the waste to cut in to free the leg.

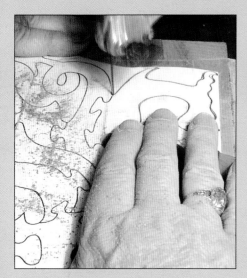

13 Cut the last leg free and remove it.

14 Cut the tail detail. Start at the base of the tail; go up and around the tail points and around the curve.

15 Following the cut line into the tail curve and around, free and discard the oval scrap piece. Carefully allow your blade to come forward out of the oval, along your previous cut line. This part can be tricky. If your cut was not absolutely vertical, you'll find yourself re-cutting a line just a hair off the original, which makes your dragon look ragged. Alternately, you can back out of the oval, turn around in the waste, back into the beginning of the oval cut line, and then go forward.

16 Continue to cut the rest of the long body piece.

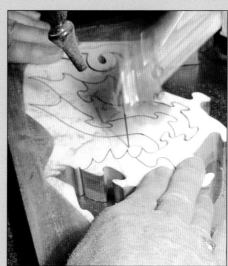

17 Notice how I cut into the waste, turned the piece 180 degrees, and then came forward to finish the last point on the body piece.

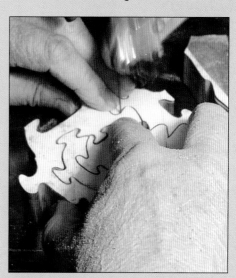

18 The final cut on the body piece. You'll see that I put my fingers quite close to the saw blade. The trick is to keep them beside the blade, not in front. I didn't get the pattern glued down well enough, so I was forced to hold the pattern down as I cut.

19 Cut along the back edge of the small wing piece, turning in the waste to finish cutting it free.

20 Cut the middle wing piece free.

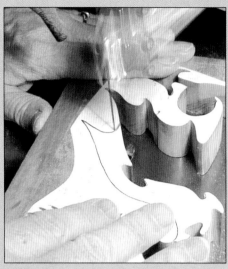

21 Then cut the upper wing piece free.

22 Finally, cut the neck piece free. Always leave plenty of scrap to hang on to.
Inset: the completed, assembled puzzle.

Puzzling it out

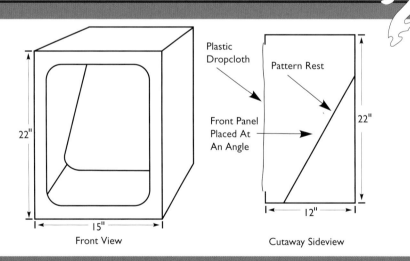

Plastic Dropcloth

Pattern Rest

Front Panel Placed At An Angle

22"

22"

15"

12"

Front View

Cutaway Sideview

Building a glue box

Take a large cardboard box (mine is about 15" wide x 22" tall x 12" deep) and tape it shut. Cut a large hole on one side. Place the cut-out piece of cardboard inside the box at an angle to use as a rest for your patterns while spraying.

I tape a piece of clear plastic drop cloth on one side, over the top of the hole. The plastic drape covers the opening. I reach in past the plastic with the can of spray adhesive in my hand. This confines most of the overspray.

Sanding and Finishing

3

Sanding

There are two reasons to sand your puzzle (or any other project). The first is to correct mistakes in cutting. With puzzles, the most common problem is that the pieces stick. This is remedied by careful sanding of the head of the key and the shoulders of the keyhole (See Figure 2 on page 4 for a diagram of key parts.). Sand lightly and test the fit. It's easy to overdo it. The second reason to sand is to improve the surface of your puzzle. I do a three-step sanding process: 1) sand the top and bottom of each piece, 2) check the cut surfaces for smoothness and gently touch up any rough spots, and 3) round over all of the edges. This process gives a professional finish to each puzzle.

Sanding and Finishing

Puzzling it out

Using a drum sander

I find that using a drum sander has cut my sanding time by 60%. If you have a relatively good surface to begin with, you can sand with only a finish grit. I usually use a 220- or 180-grit belt.

Note: There are puzzles that I cannot put through the drum sander without breaking them. I've placed a "drum sander" symbol (**O**) on the patterns in the pattern section (page 17) that can be sanded with the drum sander. You can use a drum sander on all of these patterns provided that you save the scrap and use it as a carrier. The patterns marked with the **O** symbol go through with only a rubber band around them.

To use a drum sander to sand your puzzles, follow the steps below:

- Put a rubber band completely around the outside of each puzzle. Rubber band size #64 works for most of the puzzles in this book. (See **Figure 3**.)
- If you're doing several puzzles, group them by how thick the wood is.
- Start with the group made of the thickest wood.
- Position each puzzle on the conveyor belt so that it goes through with the grain (otherwise the drum will leave visible marks).
- Run the first group through on both sides. Use one or more push sticks to support each puzzle as it goes through.
- Adjust the height of the sanding drum for the next group.

You'll have to experiment with this process. Start with some of the simpler puzzles to get the hang of it.

Figure 3. Rubber Banding the Puzzle to Prepare for Drum Sanding.

1 I like to sand the top and bottom of each piece using a drum sander. However, you can use a 5" disk sanding pad (220 grit) chucked into a drill secured by a drill stand. I used to do all of my flat sanding this way before we invested in the drum sander. Simply be careful to keep the flat sides level as you sand, and wear finger protection (See Step 6.). The only problem I've had using the disk sander in this way is occasionally sanding a piece unevenly. You will improve with practice. The top and bottom surfaces can also be sanded with an orbital or a pad sander. Rubber band the pieces together for stability and sand away. If you have a drum sander, see the "Puzzling it out" tip box, left, for more information.

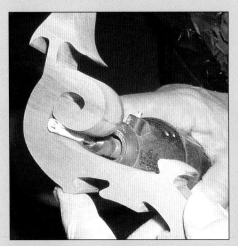

2 After sanding the top and bottom of each puzzle piece, I check the cut surfaces for smoothness. Touch up any rough places — gently — to keep the fit. I sometimes do minor touch-ups with a sanding gadget (a split mandrel) for my rotary power tool. It gets into very small places, like dragon claws and tails. See the split mandrel tip box for information on where to buy them.

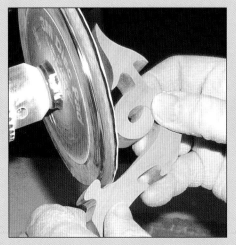

3 I use the disk sander to sand all of the outer edges of each puzzle piece. Any part that someone is likely to touch should be smooth.

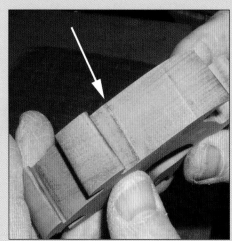

4 The arrow in the photo points to a mark on the hind leg where I started the cut to separate the leg from the body piece. (See Step 13, page 11.)

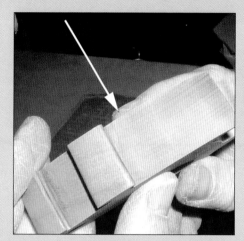

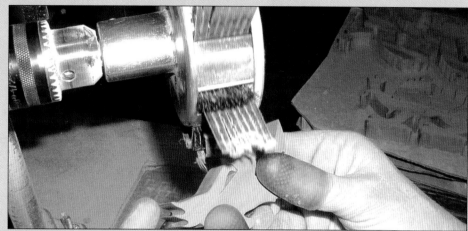

5 It's not unusual to have this kind of minor flaw. It's easy to sand out, which I have done here.

6 My last step is to round over all of the edges. Notice the rubber finger pads. Without the protection, you can take the skin off your fingers so fast! Rubber finger pads are available in several sizes at office supply stores. Rounding over the edges gives a nice finish, provides visual separation of the pieces, and sometime removes a flaw. I use a Sand-O-Flex flap sander. This gadget was designed to round over edges without gouging. I use a 240-grit scored refill and cut along the scored lines. I end up with 64 ⅛" strips of sandpaper, which can get into all the little places in the puzzle pieces. You can adjust the length of the strips for larger and smaller pieces.

Where You Can Find a Split Mandrel

When Judy wore out her first split mandrel, she couldn't find a replacement. She went to a local machine shop and had one made for her. Then we got this tip from Terry Cooper of Ottawa, Ontario, Canada. He found split mandrels in a "very small home-based carving shop" near his house. His dealer buys them from Foredom, and (if you can't find them locally) so can you. Here is their web site: **www.blackstoneind.com/foundations/store/home.asp**. If you're doing a search on the Foredom site online, enter "split mandrel" in the Search Products box. Judy recommends the M21 Mandrel for her fantasy puzzles. As of this writing it is modestly priced at $1, so buy several.

Puzzling it out

Using a carrier

I often use a carrier, made of the scrap wood I've cut away from the puzzle. To do this, I save the scrap pieces, fit them back around the puzzle, rubber band them together, and run them through with everything else. For non-landscape puzzles, I refer to the scrap pieces, which I assemble together with the actual puzzle pieces, as the "carrier." The carrier helps to avoid crunching the puzzles.

For landscape puzzles, I leave a solid piece of scrap around the outside of the entire puzzle to serve as a carrier. (The photo at the left shows the *Conflict in Clouds* puzzle.) Before taking the photo, I removed the sky pieces. They were included when I ran the puzzle through the drum sander; however, the puzzle was freshly oiled, so I removed the pieces to prevent the oil from the surrounding pieces to bleed into the unoiled sky pieces. You'll still get a good idea of what the puzzle looks like with the carrier in place.

Finishing

The General Finishing Process

Because I usually want the actual wood colors to come through, I use Danish oil in Natural to finish my puzzles. I've had good luck with the General Finishes brand.

Color on most of the exotic woods will change over time as a result of exposure to ultraviolet rays. Because of this, when I want the color to hold, I use a clear, UV-blocking Danish oil on these woods. The "tech guy" I spoke to at the company that makes this oil told me that the oil will double the life of the color. General Finishes sells this product under the "Outdoor Oil" label.

Because making and selling puzzles is my business, I do a lot of oiling. I start by pouring the oil into a one-gallon, resealable freezer bag. Next, I disassemble the puzzle and drop the pieces into the oil. I let them sit in the oil for a short time, and then remove them from the oil. As soon as they're out of the bag of oil, I place them on plastic trays lined with paper towels to drip dry.

Most of the pieces dry completely without wiping, but I inspect all of the pieces and wipe as necessary. The more cut-line detail there is in a puzzle piece, the more attention it needs at this step. The extra attention is necessary for these pieces because more oil gets into the cut line than can be absorbed by the surfaces inside the cut. Then, the oil bleeds out, usually over several hours.

After drying all of the pieces that need it, I reassemble the puzzle and let it air-dry overnight. Remember that oil fumes are extremely volatile. I dry the pieces with paper towels because paper towels dry quickly and completely. I dispose of the paper towels by dropping them *loosely* into a large paper bag and letting them dry overnight. This process permits no buildup of fumes to cause spontaneous combustion. The important thing is *not* to stuff them tightly into a plastic bag.

Finishing of the *Conflict in Clouds* puzzle

I finished this puzzle with Cherry and Golden Fruitwood stains, as well as with Danish oil in Natural. I used Behlen stains, and the color names are the ones they use. Do a little experimenting to find your favorites.

The Golden Fruitwood color, as it came out of the bottle, was a little too orange for my taste. I darkened it with a little Cherry stain. I dipped the pieces of the dragons and the pieces representing the water in the stain, wiped them immediately, and set them out to dry (on the paper-towel-lined plastic trays, as noted before).

I dipped the pieces representing the mountains and the ground in Cherry stain and wiped them immediately. After all of the stained pieces were dry, I dipped them in Danish oil in Natural and let them dry.

For the clouds and the pieces representing the base, I used Danish oil in Natural. I left the sky pieces unoiled.

With landscape puzzles that I expect children to play with, I oil all of the pieces. Bare wood picks up fingerprints because it does not have the oil to protect it.

The Patterns

4

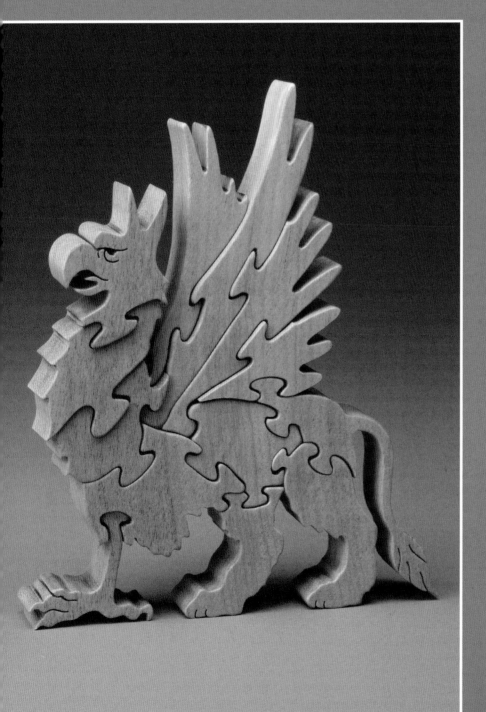

On the following pages, you'll find a selection of my fantasy patterns. The patterns are grouped by ease of cutting, but I like to group them by subject as well. (Check out the Index on page 76 for different groupings.) For instance, *Cutie Pie, T.D.C., Wanna Play?*, and the *Hatchling* are the fat-bellied baby dragons. They're surprisingly popular.

The gargoyles comprise another group. They are all based on gargoyles found at Notre Dame in Paris. Still another group are the patterns from Greek mythology. This group includes the *Centaur, Griffin, Mermaid, Pegasus, Unicorn, Hippogriff, Hydra,* and *Phoenix.*

Fleet and *Slim* make up a small group of their own. These are the dragons I designed specifically to use those beautiful, odd, little leftover bits of wood that I used to throw away. They are easy to adapt to the wood available. You can shorten or lengthen them, or reposition the wing or tail to suit the scrap.

I've also included two landscape puzzles. For the backgrounds, I use mountains, sky pieces, clouds, or any combination of these. The keys are tree shapes, either attached at the base or as separate pieces, as well as the more usual shapes. You need a ground line—either an actual one or a mental one—on which to place the elements of your design.

Modifying the patterns

Any of the patterns in this book can be enlarged. They probably should be enlarged if you want to give them to children under the age of 3. Once you get comfortable cutting the patterns, try experimenting and creating your own designs.

An easy way to begin modifying patterns is to change the shape of dragon's eyes. Make the eyes large and rounded for a "happy" expression or make them small and pointed for a "fierce" expression. You should also change the slant of the mouth line up or down to go with the eyes. The illustration below shows two versions of the same dragon head to convey these points.

Puzzling it out

Lumberspeak

■ **Grain Figures.** "Figured," "fiddleback," "quilted," "wavy," "flame crotch," etc. are terms that really mean that the grain of the wood is not straight.

■ **Hardwood and softwood.** "Hardwood" only means "deciduous tree," or a tree that loses its leaves in the fall. It has nothing to do with how hard the wood is. Some hardwoods are softer (less dense, lighter) than some softwoods.

■ **Maple and oak.** Lumber people know only two kinds of maple, hard and soft, and only two kinds of oak, red and white. This is the case regardless of the fact that there are 20 or 30 species of each.

■ **Hardwood sizes.** Hardwoods are sold by the quarter inch, i.e., ¾" (three-quarter), ⁵⁄₄" (five-quarter), etc. This is the unplaned measurement. Planing reduces the thickness of the board. If you go to specialty lumberyards, they will plane to your specifications, for a price.

■ **Skip planing.** Hardwood lumber dealers will usually skip plane your lumber if you ask them to do so. This type of planing will give you the thickest board possible. However, you will have to pay more attention when you sand to make sure everything is smooth.

■ **Kerf.** This refers to the wood taken out by the saw blade.

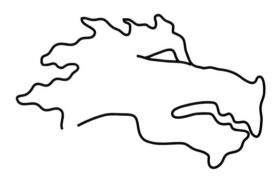

Happy Dragon   **Fierce Dragon**

These two dragon faces have been modified to change their expressions. The dragon on the left has a more friendly or happy look. The dragon on the right seems fierce or sad.

The Practice Pattern is simply a running line that forms the
shapes, curves, points, eyes, teeth, and so forth found in
my puzzles. So practice!

Easy Patterns

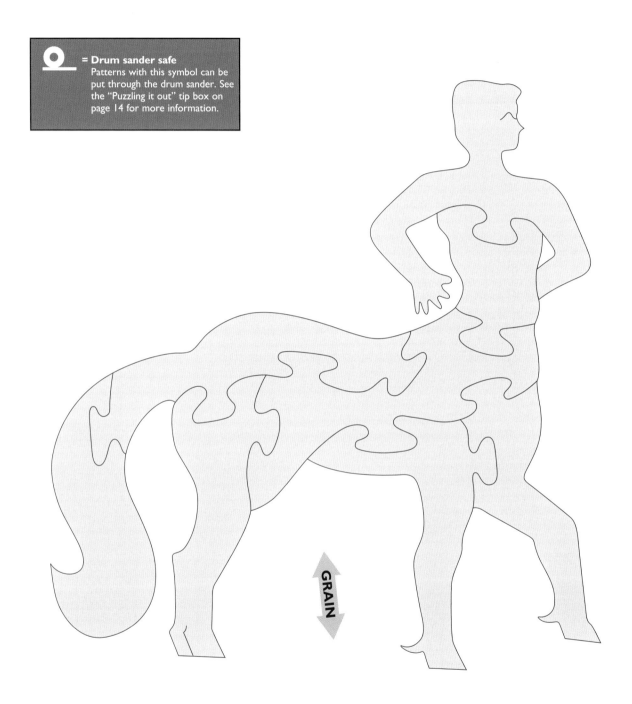

= **Drum sander safe**
Patterns with this symbol can be put through the drum sander. See the "Puzzling it out" tip box on page 14 for more information.

GRAIN

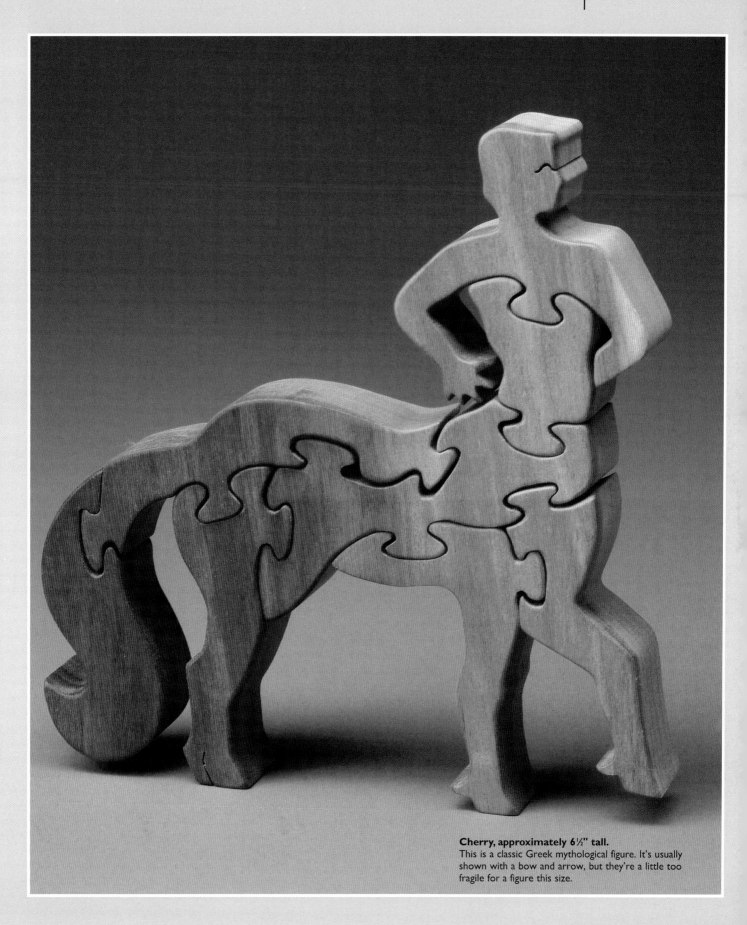

Cherry, approximately 6½" tall.
This is a classic Greek mythological figure. It's usually shown with a bow and arrow, but they're a little too fragile for a figure this size.

GRAIN

Chakte Kok, approximately 6" tall.
This was the first of the fat-bellied baby dragons and was so popular that I did more baby dragons.

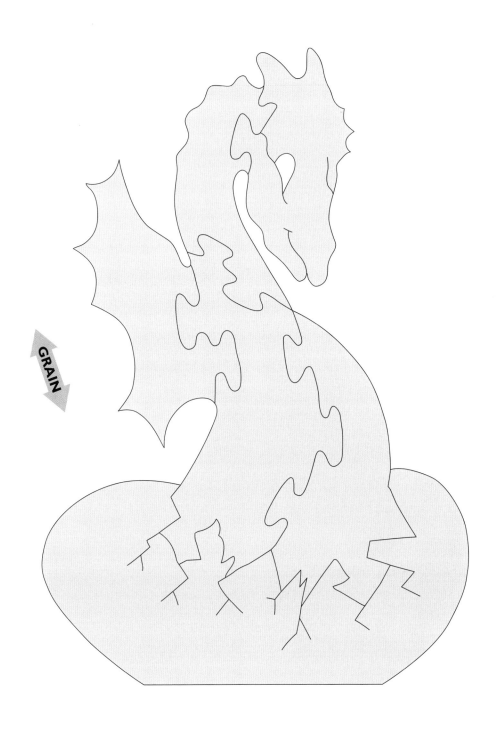

GRAIN

Cherry, approximately 7" tall.
Another of the babies—this one is based loosely
on the shape of the *Lambton Worm* from Lora S. Irish's
Great Book of Dragon Patterns.

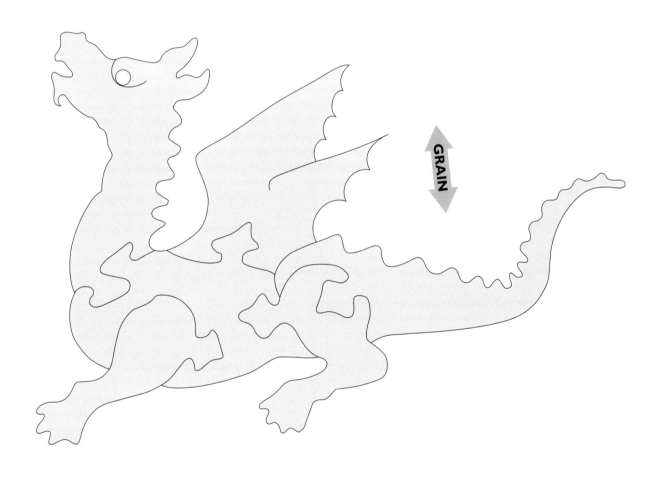

GRAIN

Peroba rosa, approximately 5" tall.
I was running out of names, so I borrowed from a line in a poem
by Lewis Carroll, "He would answer to Hie or to any loud cry."
Call him anything you like; this is a very popular pattern.

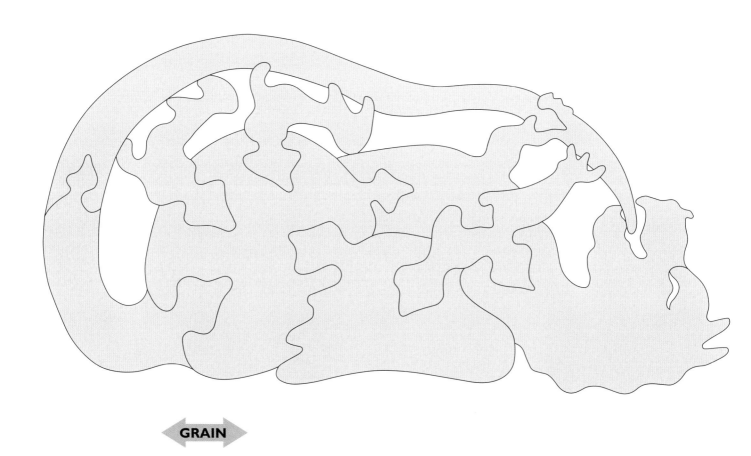

GRAIN

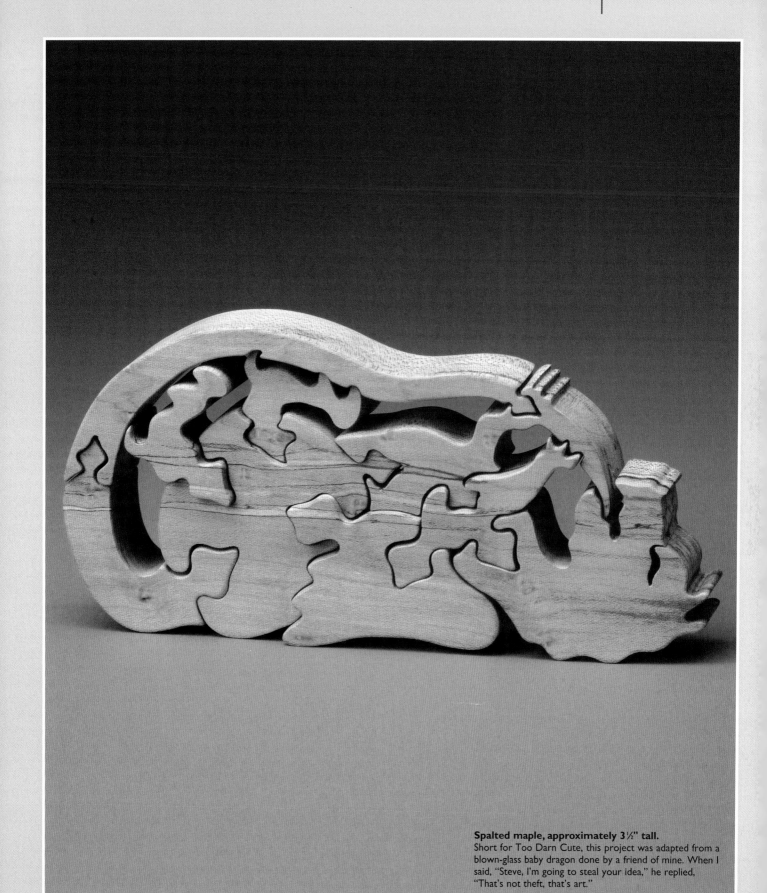

Spalted maple, approximately 3½" tall.
Short for Too Darn Cute, this project was adapted from a
blown-glass baby dragon done by a friend of mine. When I
said, "Steve, I'm going to steal your idea," he replied,
"That's not theft, that's art."

GRAIN

Black walnut, approximately 6" tall.
Another of the babies. I think this one is about four years old with no one to play with.

GRAIN

A "scrap" dragon. These dragons look different depending on the wood used.

Chakte kok, approximately 2½" tall.

Satinwood, approximately 2½" tall.

GRAIN

Gargoyle, Pensive

Spalted cherry, approximately 6" tall.
He looks like he's thinking things over.
He's the most popular of the three gargoyles.

GRAIN

Chakte kok, approximately 5½" tall.
Keeping an eye on things.

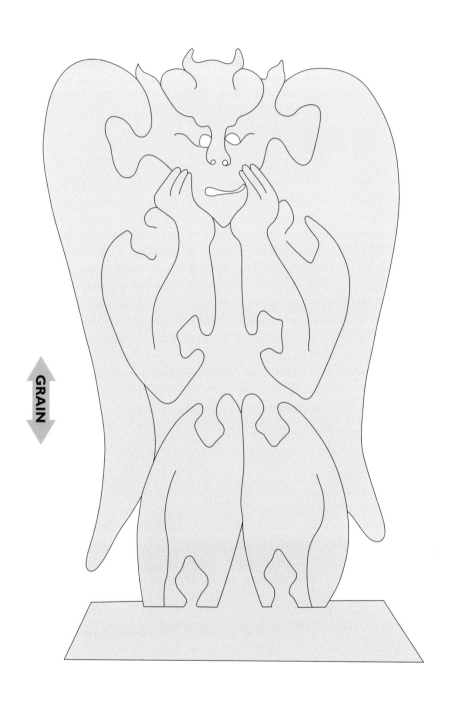

GRAIN

Cherry, approximately 6" tall.
He does look like he's got a problem.
Watch the face and fingers on this one.

GRAIN

Satinwood, approximately 8" tall.
Another of the mythological figures, this creature has the head, wings, and front legs of an eagle and the body, hind legs, and tail of a lion.

GRAIN

Lacewood, approximately 7½" tall.
This is an adaptation of the *Laughing Dragon* (see page 62.)

GRAIN

Aspen, approximately 6½" tall.
Another classic mythological creature. She sits
on her rock, combing her long hair.

GRAIN

Maple, approximately 8" tall.
This is the Greek winged horse. He is traditionally white.
The rippled figure in the wood is the true "fiddleback"
pattern that guitar and violin makers look for. The presence
of this pattern signifies that the wood resonates.

GRAIN

Bird's-eye maple, approximately 5" tall.
Another classic shape. Both this and Pegasus are cut from pieces of maple I bought from an art show customer. A man came up to me at a show, and asked, "Do you buy wood?" Silly question!

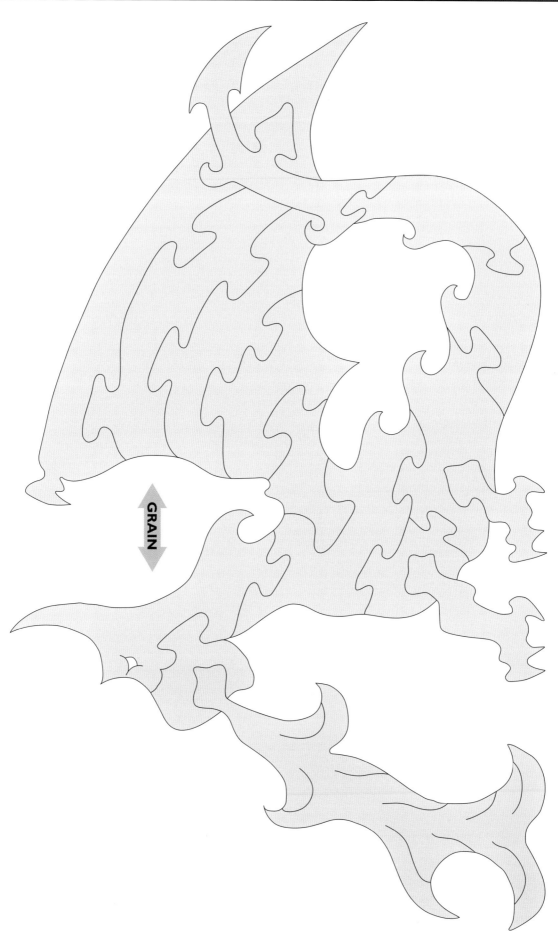

GRAIN

Macacaubo, approximately 5½" tall.
He's named for his flame. The wood is pronounced "mah-cah-cah-WHY-bo." It's South American, and one of the lesser known woods.

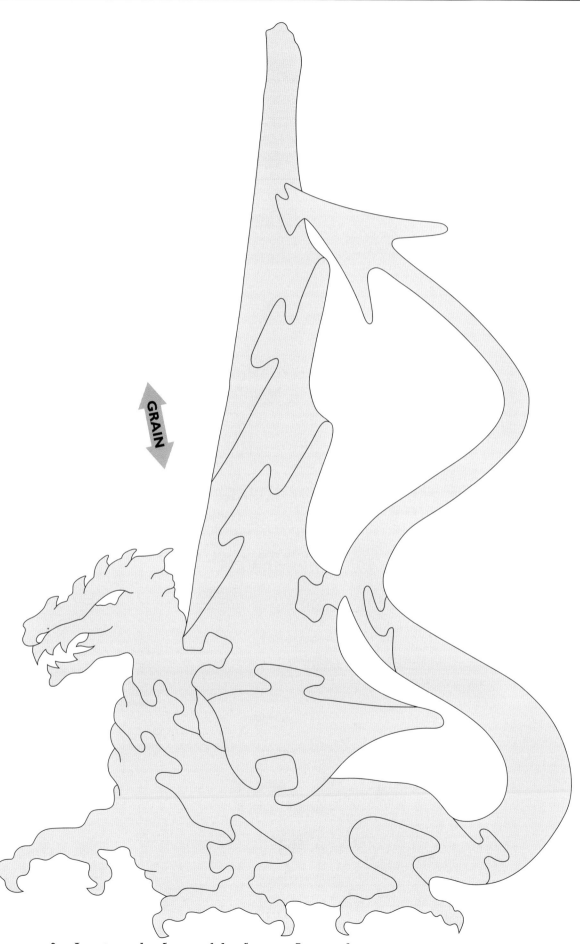

GRAIN

Chakte Kok, approximately 9" tall.
This one was adapted from a pewter pendant about an inch and a half tall.

Helpful Cutting Hints: Start by drilling a hole through one of the eyes. Insert your blade through the hole and re-attach it. Tighten the tension. Cut the eye shape and follow the cut line to the other eye and cut it. Cut down and around the nose shape. Back out to the point where the nose line touches the moustache and cut the moustache free. Release the blade, take it out of the interior cuts, and start on the leaves. I generally take out the top five leaves, then the eyebrows, and then the face. The rest of it is easier.

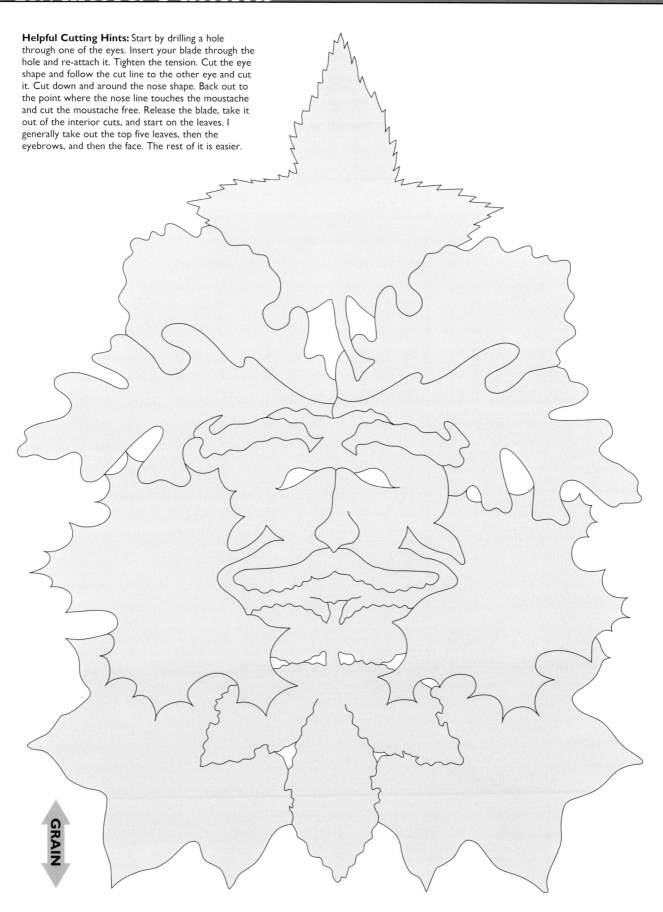

GRAIN

Bocote, approximately 9" tall.
This is traditionally done from all oak leaves, but I chose to use a variety of leaves—sweet gum, burr oak, white oak, maple, tulip poplar, and hickory—with willow leaves for the eyebrows and a maple seed for the moustache. I left the face piece unoiled to emphasize the face peering out from the trees. This is the most difficult of the fantasy puzzles in this book, because of the points of the maple leaves and the interior cuts in the face.

Photocopy at 105%

GRAIN

Black walnut with sapwood, approximately 10" tall.
This is another mythological construct. It has the head,
front legs, and wings of an eagle and the body, hind legs,
and tail of a horse.

GRAIN

Photocopy at 105%

Walnut, approximately 7" tall.
This is yet another creature from Greek mythology.
My multi-headed sea creature has only three heads, but
you can add as many as you wish.

GRAIN

Peroba rosa, approximately 10" tall.
This one is from Chinese mythology. Chinese dragons are
wingless and only Imperial Dragons have five claws.

GRAIN

Walnut, approximately 5" tall.
This one is adapted from a dragon designed by one of my
customers, a Year of the Dragon lady.

GRAIN

Bubinga, approximately 8" tall.
Another dragon adapted from Lora S. Irish's designs.
Can you spot the right one?

GRAIN

Note: If you're going to use a drum sander on this one, do the flames and the body separately.

Padauk and bird's-eye maple, approximately 8" tall.
The phoenix dies in flame and is reborn from its ashes.
The idea is common to several mythologies.

GRAIN

Aspen, approximately 9" tall.
A more active version of the Unicorn. This one is
cut from aspen, the whitest wood I can afford.

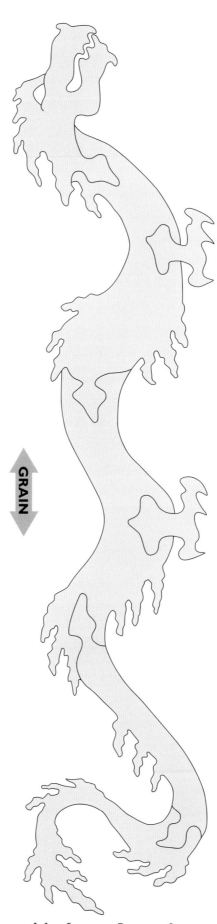

GRAIN

Chakte kok, approximately 2" tall.
The second pattern for bits of wood I used to throw away.

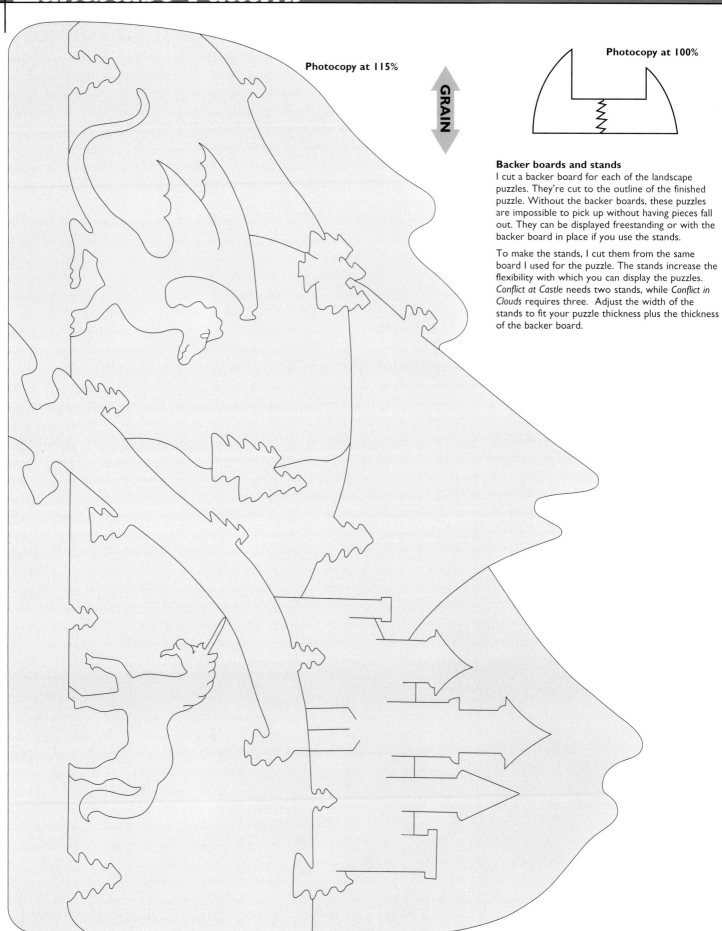

Photocopy at 115%

GRAIN

Photocopy at 100%

Backer boards and stands

I cut a backer board for each of the landscape puzzles. They're cut to the outline of the finished puzzle. Without the backer boards, these puzzles are impossible to pick up without having pieces fall out. They can be displayed freestanding or with the backer board in place if you use the stands.

To make the stands, I cut them from the same board I used for the puzzle. The stands increase the flexibility with which you can display the puzzles. *Conflict at Castle* needs two stands, while *Conflict in Clouds* requires three. Adjust the width of the stands to fit your puzzle thickness plus the thickness of the backer board.

Cherry with Baltic birch backer board, approximately 8" tall.
In this castlescape, I used the base pieces and the path up the hill to the castle as the ground lines. The dragon, unicorn, and castle are placed on the ground lines. When designing, fill in the background with whatever seems appropriate. You can change the elements easily. For instance, take out the unicorn and put in St. George.

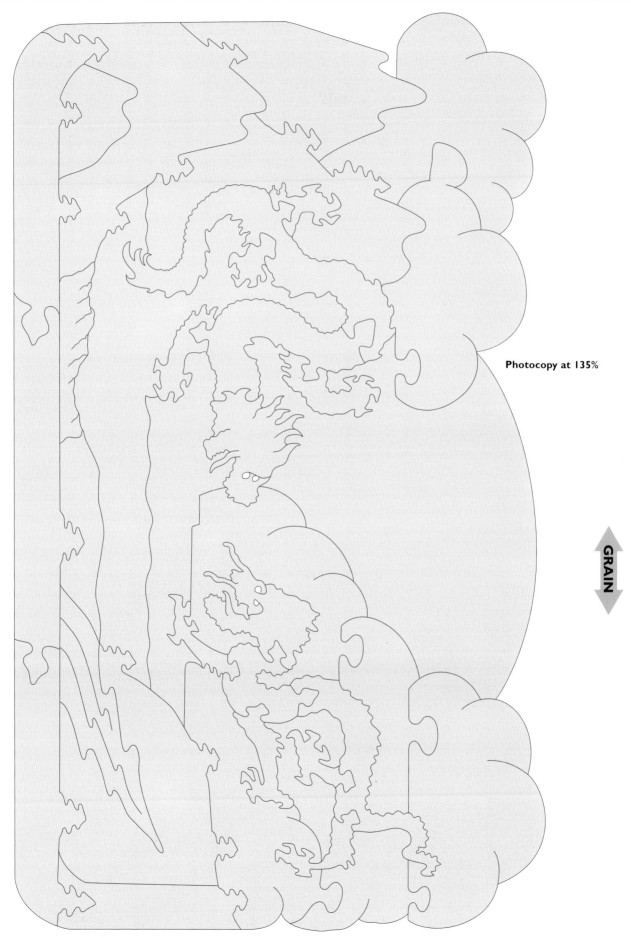

Photocopy at 135%

GRAIN

Cherry with Baltic birch backer board, approximately 9" tall.
Traditionally, Chinese dragons are river or lake dragons or sky or cloud dragons. Therefore, although there's a ground line, all of the action is above it. I did place the dragons on the same level; I wanted one to appear to be descending from the cloud, while the other rose from the lake. I've used all of the background elements—sky, clouds, and mountains.

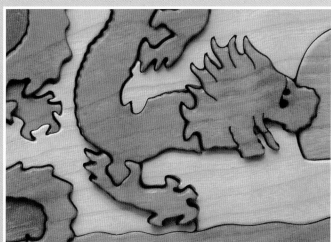

Index

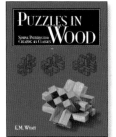
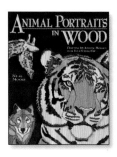